First Facts®

Transportation Zone

Ambulances in Action

by Anne E. Hanson

CAPSTONE PRESS
a capstone imprint

First Facts is published by Capstone Press,
151 Good Counsel Drive, P.O. Box 669, Mankato, Minnesota 56002.
www.capstonepub.com

 Books published by Capstone Press are manufactured with paper
containing at least 10 percent post-consumer waste.

Library of Congress Cataloging-in-Publication Data
Hanson, Anne E.
  Ambulances in action / by Anne E. Hanson.
      p. cm. — (First facts. Transportation zone)
  Includes bibliographical references and index.
  Summary: Describes the history, equipment, and parts of an ambulance.
  ISBN 978-1-4296-6827-9 (library binding)
  1. Ambulances—Juvenile literature. 2. Ambulance service—Juvenile
literature. I. Title.
  TL235.8.H36 2012
  629.222'34—dc22   2011006032

Editorial Credits
Karen L. Daas and Brenda Haugen, editors; Gene Bentdahl, designer; Eric Gohl, media
      researcher; Laura Manthe, production specialist

Image Credits
BigStockPhoto.com/Mary Losh, 1
Bridgeman Art Library/Archives Charmet/Musee du Val-de-Grace, Paris,
      France, 9
Capstone Studio/Karon Dubke, 22
Corbis/Bettmann, 6
Dreamstime/Monkey Business Images, 16; Roberto Marinello, 15
Getty Images Inc./Topical Press Agency, 11; Stone/Dennis O'Clair, cover
iStockphoto/tillsonburg, 19; Tim McCaig, 5
Shutterstock/Monkey Business Images, 12; Pawel Nawrot, 21

Printed in the United States of America in North Mankato, Minnesota.
032011   006110CGF11

Table of Contents

Ambulances

A vehicle speeds by with its lights flashing. Its siren blares. It's an ambulance rushing a sick or hurt person to a hospital. The lights and siren warn drivers to move out of the way. The **patient** receives medical help on the way to the hospital. An ambulance helps save lives.

patient: someone who receives medical care

Before Ambulances

Before ambulances, sick or hurt people had to wait longer for help to arrive. Doctors traveled on foot or by horses to homes. Friends or family members took sick people to hospitals. Wounded soldiers waited on battlefields for nurses to reach them.

Inventor of the Ambulance

Baron Dominique Jean Larrey was a doctor in France. He invented the first ambulance in 1792. The horse-drawn cart could carry two people at a time. Many cities used ambulances based on Larrey's design.

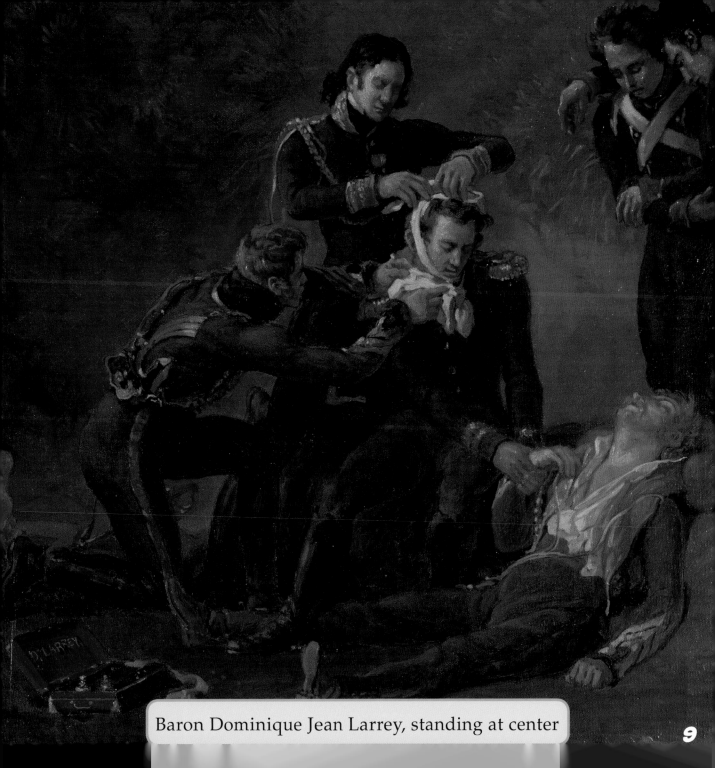

Baron Dominique Jean Larrey, standing at center

Ambulance Crews

Emergency medical technicians (EMTs) and **paramedics** drive ambulances. They also care for patients. Ambulance crews treat people in their homes or at accident scenes. They continue to give care as they take people to hospitals.

emergency medical technician: a person trained to help sick or hurt people during emergencies

paramedic: a person who treats sick and hurt people

Inside an Ambulance

Crews care for patients inside ambulances. They may have the patient lie on a **stretcher**. Crews use medical equipment. Some of this equipment measures a patient's **blood pressure** and breathing. Medical supplies are stored in cabinets in the ambulance.

stretcher: a piece of equipment used to carry someone who is sick or injured

blood pressure: the force of blood pulsing against the walls of the arteries when the heart is pumping and when it is at rest

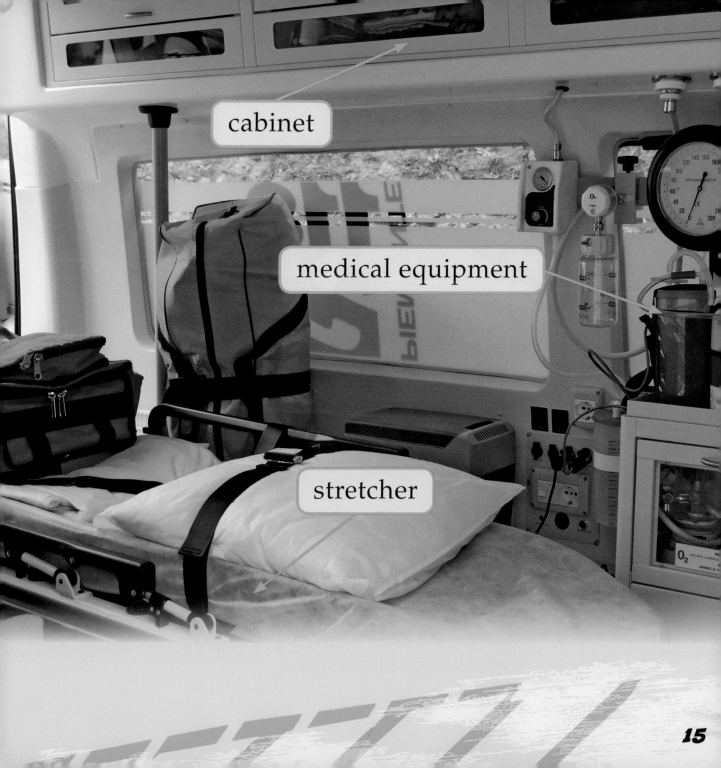

cabinet

medical equipment

stretcher

How an Ambulance Works

Ambulances are powered by **diesel engines**. The driver controls the ambulance with a steering wheel and brakes. Drivers use buttons to turn on the siren and lights. White lights help the crew see inside the ambulance at night. Batteries power medical equipment.

diesel engine: a type of engine that burns heavy oil to make power

Ambulance Rescue Today

When an emergency happens, an ambulance rushes to the scene. The crew treats sick or injured people. They call the hospital. They tell doctors about a patient's injuries. At the hospital, doctors and nurses care for the patient.

Ambulance Facts

- The word ambulance is printed backward on the front of an ambulance. This is so other drivers can read this word in their rearview mirrors.

- Ambulances have big windows in back. The windows keep riders from getting carsick.

- Ambulances have crash bars near the bottom of the vehicle. These bumpers protect the ambulance in narrow areas such as alleys.

- The rear bumper of an ambulance flips down. EMTs and paramedics can then roll stretchers close to the ambulance. They can place the stretcher in the ambulance more easily.

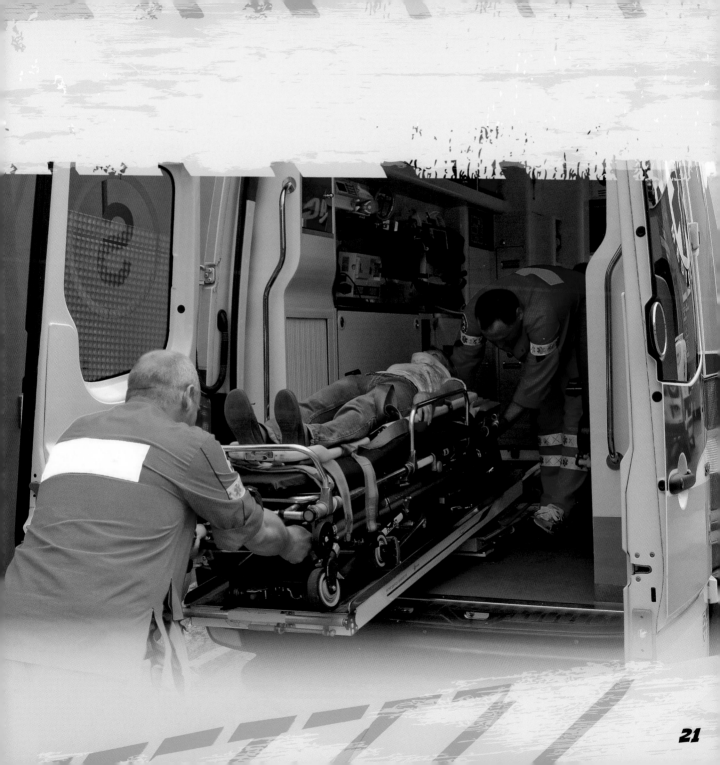

Hands On: Check Your Pulse

EMTs and paramedics help people who are hurt. They check a patient's pulse to see how fast blood is pumping through the body. You can check your pulse.

What You Need

watch or clock

What You Do

1. Gently place two fingers on the left side of your neck. You should feel your pulse. Your pulse throbs as your heart beats. Each beat moves blood through your body.
2. Look at a watch or clock. Count how many times your heart beats in six seconds.
3. Add a zero to the end of the number. This number is how many times your heart beats in one minute.
4. Run in place for one minute.
5. Repeat steps 2 and 3.

Your heart beats faster when you are active. It also beats more if you are scared or hurt. EMTs and paramedics can tell how fast patients' hearts are beating by taking their pulses.

Glossary

blood pressure (BLUHD PRE-shuhr)—the force of blood pulsing against the walls of the arteries when the heart is pumping and when it is at rest

diesel engine (DEE-zuhl EN-juhn)—a type of engine that burns heavy oil to make power

emergency medical technician (i-MUHR-juhn-see MED-uh-kuhl tek-NISH-uhn)—a person trained to help sick or hurt people during emergencies

paramedic (pa-ruh-MEH-dik)—a person who treats sick and hurt people

patient (PAY-shunt)—someone who receives medical care

stretcher (STRECH-ur)—a piece of equipment used to carry someone who is sick or injured

Read More

Amoroso, Gary M. and Cynthia A. Klingel. *Ambulances*. Machines at Work. Chanhassen, Minn.: Child's World, 2007.

Manolis, Kay. *Ambulances*. Mighty Machines. Minneapolis: Bellwether Media, 2008.

Waxman, Laura Hamilton. *Ambulances on the Move*. Vroom-Vroom. Minneapolis: Lerner Publications Co., 2011.

Internet Sites

FactHound offers a safe, fun way to find Internet sites related to this book. All of the sites on FactHound have been researched by our staff.

Here's all you do:

Visit *www.facthound.com*

Type in this code: 9781429668279

Check out projects, games and lots more at
www.capstonekids.com

Index